KT-199-056

A TWIST OF TALES

A TWIST OF TALES

JULIA DONALDSON

WITH ILLUSTRATIONS BY
PETER BAILEY

Barrington Stoke

First published in 2016 in Great Britain by
Barrington Stoke Ltd
18 Walker Street, Edinburgh, EH3 7LP

www.barringtonstoke.co.uk

'The Strange Dream' and 'The King's Ears' were first published
as individual books by Oxford University Press (2000) and 'Clever
Katya' was first published as an individual book by Ginn (1999)

Text © 1999 & 2000 Julia Donaldson
Illustrations © 2016 Peter Bailey

A CIP catalogue record for this book is available
from the British Library upon request

ISBN: 978-1-78112-570-0

Printed in China by Leo

This book is super readable for young readers beginning
their independent reading journey.

For mums, dads and other grown-ups

Learning to read alone is a big step for
your child. Rather like those first steps
back in the toddler years, it helps to have
a trusted adult to lend a helping hand.
Julia Donaldson is a much-loved storyteller
for the very young and here she tells three
stories in clear and accessible language
to help your little reader set out on a
wonderful reading journey.

CONTENTS

THE KING'S EARS

King March had a tall gold crown. He
wore it all the time.

He wore it when he ate.

He wore it when he danced.

He even wore it in bed.

"The King must love that crown," the people said.

But King March didn't love his crown. It was hot and it was heavy.

So why did he wear it?

He wore it because it hid his ears.

King March's ears were his big secret. They were not like your ears or my ears. They were long and furry, like a horse's ears.

The only person who had ever seen King March's ears was Owen. Owen was the man who cut the King's hair. The King made Owen promise not to tell anyone about his long furry ears.

"I promise," Owen said.

It was hard for Owen to keep his promise.

'I wish I could tell just one person,' Owen thought. 'I wish I could tell my wife Alis.'

Alis could see that Owen was not happy.

"What's the matter?" she asked.

"Nothing," Owen said.

The secret seemed to grow and grow inside Owen's head. It felt heavy, as heavy as the King's tall gold crown.

Owen's head began to hurt.

He grew thin and pale.

"You're not well, Owen," Alis said. "Go and see the doctor."

So Owen went to see the doctor.

"What's the matter?" the doctor asked.

Owen told the doctor that he had a secret.

"This secret is making me ill," he said. "I have promised not to tell it to anyone, but if I don't tell someone I feel as if I will die."

The doctor told Owen what to do.

"You must go for a long walk," he said. "You must walk out of the town and into the country. When you come to a place where there are no people, no

animals and no birds you can whisper your secret to the air. Then you will feel better."

Owen did what the doctor said.

He went for a long walk.

He walked out of town and into the country.

After a long time he came to a place where lots of rushes grew. There were no people, no animals and no birds. Owen stood still and he whispered his secret.

"King March has horse's ears," he whispered.

And all at once Owen felt happy. He ran back home.

"You look better," Alis said.

"I feel better," said Owen. "Much better."

Time passed. The rushes grew longer.

King March's hair grew longer too. He sent for Owen to cut it.

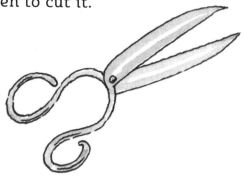

Owen sang as he cut the King's hair.

"You seem happy," the King said. "Do you like dancing as well as singing?"

"Yes," said Owen.

"Good," the King said. "Then you must come to the dance in my palace next week. I have asked a band of pipers to come and play."

The band lived a long way from King March's palace. As they walked to the palace, they came to the place where the rushes grew.

"Look at these tall rushes," one of the pipers said. "Let's make some new pipes out of them."

They cut some of the rushes and made them into pipes. Then they went on their way.

That night the King's palace was full of people. They ate and drank. They talked and laughed.

"Now it's time to dance," said King March. He called to the band. "Play us a tune!"

The band picked up their new pipes. They tried to play. But no tune came out of the pipes.

Instead, the pipes began to whisper.

"King March has horse's ears," the pipes whispered.

Everyone looked at King March. He went red. Then he sighed. "It's true," he said. "My secret's out." And he took off his tall gold crown.

Everyone could see the King's ears. They were long and furry.

"Now you can all have a good laugh," King March said.

But no one laughed.

King March was a good king and everyone liked him. It didn't matter what his ears looked like.

All at once King March felt happy.
He put his tall crown down on the table.

"Now I won't need to wear it all the
time," he said.

The King called to the band again.
"See if you can play a tune now!"

The band picked up their pipes.
This time a merry tune came out, and
everyone danced.

King March danced, and so did Owen
and Alis.

King March whispered in Owen's ear,
"Come and cut my hair tomorrow."

Owen felt scared when he went to the palace the next day. But King March didn't look cross.

"Did you tell my secret to anyone?" the King asked, as Owen cut his hair.

"No," said Owen. But he told the King how he had whispered the secret to the rushes.

"The band must have made some of those rushes into pipes," Owen said.

"So that's how my secret got out," said King March.

King March laughed. Owen laughed too. They both felt happy.

"No more secrets," said King March.

"No more secrets," said Owen.

THE STRANGE DREAM

Kate and Colin lived in a village by the sea. They had a little white house and a garden with a plum tree in it. Kate worked in the garden, and Colin went out fishing on a boat.

One stormy night, Kate had a strange dream.

"I dreamed that I was standing on London Bridge," she told Colin. "There were lots of little shops on the bridge. A man with a long grey beard came out of one of the shops and told me some good news."

"What was the news?" Colin asked.

"I can't remember!" said Kate. "But maybe we'll have some good luck now."

But Kate was wrong.

The storm had blown all the plums off the tree. They were lying on the ground, squashed.

"I can't sell those," said Kate.

"And it's too stormy to go out fishing," said Colin.

The wind blew all day and all the next night.

In the morning, Kate said to Colin, "I had that dream again. I was on London Bridge, and a man with a long grey beard told me some good news."

"What news?" Colin asked.

"I still can't remember," said Kate. "But I'm sure we'll have some good luck today."

But she was wrong.

When Colin went down to the sea he found that his boat had been smashed in the storm.

"Now I can't go fishing," he said. "And we don't have any money to buy a new boat."

"Never mind," said Kate. "We'll think of something."

That night Kate had the same dream again. In the morning she packed up some food and clothes.

"Where are you going?" Colin asked.

"To London Bridge," said Kate. "I'm going to see the man with the long grey beard."

"Don't be silly," said Colin. "That was just a dream. Dreams don't come true."

"We'll see," said Kate, and she set off for London.

Kate walked all day. At night she slept under a hedge. Next day she came to London Bridge. It had lots of little shops on it, just like in her dream.

Kate stood on the bridge. People went into the shops and came out again, but no one spoke to Kate. She stood there a long time.

It began to grow dark.

'Colin was right,' Kate thought. 'Dreams don't come true. I'd better go home.'

Just then a man came out of a shop. He saw Kate standing there.

"Can I help you?" he asked.

Kate looked up. She jumped.

The man had a long grey beard. He was the man from her dream!

"Do you have any news for me?" Kate asked.

"No," said the man. "Why should I?"

"Oh dear," said Kate. Then she told him about her dream.

The man laughed.

"Fancy coming to London just because of a dream!" he said. "Dreams don't come true."

Then the man smiled. "I had a strange dream, too," he said. "I dreamed that I was in a village by the sea. There was a white house with a plum tree in the garden, but all the plums were on

the ground. I was digging under the plum tree. I dug and dug, and in the end I dug up a pot of gold!"

The man shook his head. "It was just a silly dream," he said. "I'm not going to try to find that village and I'm not going to dig under a plum tree. I told you. Dreams don't come true."

"You're right," said Kate. "I am silly. I'd better go home."

But there was a big smile on her face.

The man said goodbye to Kate and walked away.

Kate didn't walk away. She ran. She ran all night.

"I must get home and tell Colin," she said.

When Kate got home, Colin was digging in the garden.

"Well?" he said. "Did you hear any good news?"

"Yes!" said Kate. "Give me that spade!"

Just then, the spade hit something hard. Kate dug it up. It was a big round pot.

Kate took the pot out of the earth. She took the lid off.

The pot was full of gold coins.

"Look at all that gold!" said Kate. "Some dreams really do come true!"

THE
CLEVER
GIRL

The Tsar of Russia was out in his coach
when he saw a farmer eating some
bread.

"I'm hungry," the Tsar said. "Stop
the coach!"

He got out and asked the farmer for
some bread. The farmer bowed low and
gave him some.

"This is the best bread I have ever tasted," said the Tsar. "Who made it?"

"My daughter Katya, Your Majesty," the farmer replied.

"Tell me about Katya," said the Tsar.

"Oh, she's a wonderful girl," the farmer said. "So pretty, so good, so strong, such a good worker, such a good singer ..."

"And such a good baker," the Tsar said with his mouth full of bread. "Is she clever too?"

"Oh yes," the farmer boasted. "She's the cleverest person in Russia."

"What? Cleverer than me?" asked the Tsar.

"Oh no, Your Majesty. I'm sorry, I didn't mean that ..." the farmer began.

But the Tsar had jumped back into his coach.

"I'll be back!" he called out.

The next day the Tsar came back. He gave the farmer a basket of eggs.

"If your Katya is so clever, see if she can hatch these eggs into chickens," he said. "I'll be back tomorrow!"

The farmer took the eggs to Katya.

"But these eggs are hard boiled," she said. "They won't ever hatch out."

"Oh no!" said the farmer. "What shall we do?"

"Don't worry, I know what to do," Katya said with a smile.

The next day the Tsar was on his way back to the farmer's house when he saw a girl throwing some beans onto the ground. She was singing a song.

"Grow, beans, grow!" she sang.

The Tsar stopped the coach.

"What is your name?" he asked the girl.

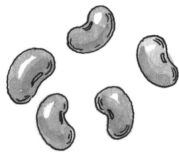

"Katya," she replied.

"So you're Clever Katya," the Tsar said. "What are you doing?"

"I'm sowing boiled beans, Your Majesty," Katya said, and she went on with her song.

The Tsar laughed. "How can boiled beans grow, you silly girl?" he asked.

"They can grow just as fast as hard-boiled eggs can hatch out," Katya replied.

The Tsar laughed again. "That's a clever reply," he said. "I thought I could trick you, but you were too clever for me. All right, you win this time, but let's see if you can do something else."

"What's that?" asked Katya.

The Tsar gave her a handful of wool.

"I want you to make curtains for the palace out of this," he said.

Katya took the wool home and told her father what she had done.

"Oh no," said the farmer. "How can you make curtains with so little wool? It's impossible."

"Don't worry, Father," Katya replied. "I'll think of something."

The next day the Tsar came back to the house. He was beginning to like Katya.

"Well?" he asked. "Have you made the curtains?"

Katya smiled and gave him a little twig.

"What's this for?" the Tsar asked.

"Well, Your Majesty, it's like this," Katya said. "We're very poor – too poor to buy a spinning wheel. But if you can make a spinning wheel out of this twig, then I can spin the wool and make your curtains."

The Tsar laughed. He knew he couldn't make a spinning wheel out of a little twig.

"You win again," he said.

Katya laughed too. She was beginning to like the Tsar.

"There's one more thing I want you to do," the Tsar said, and he gave Katya a cup. "I want you to fill this cup with all the water from the sea," he said.

Katya told her father what she had to do.

"But that's impossible," he said.

"Don't worry," Katya replied. "I'll think of something."

The next day the Tsar was back. Katya came to the door with the cup.

"It's empty!" the Tsar said. "You're not so clever after all. You can't do what I asked."

"Yes, I can," Katya replied. "I can fill the cup with all the water from the sea, but there's one problem."

"What's that?" asked the Tsar.

"Well," Katya said, "if I do that, then all the rivers will flow into the sea and fill it up again. But if you dam up all the rivers first, then I can fill the cup with water from the sea."

The Tsar laughed louder than ever. He knew he couldn't dam up all the rivers.

"You're a very clever girl," he said. "Will you marry me?"

"I will if you promise me one thing," said Katya.

"What's that?" the Tsar asked.

"Promise me that if you ever get fed up with me and send me back home, you will let me take one thing with me."

"What thing?" the Tsar asked.

"The thing I love best in the palace," Katya replied.

"I promise," said the Tsar.

So Katya married the Tsar, and for a year they lived happily. But one night the Tsar was in a bad mood and he quarrelled with Katya.

"You think you're so clever," he said. "Well, you can go back and be clever in your father's house."

He called his servants and told them to get a cart ready to take Katya home.

All Katya said was, "You look tired. Have a cushion for your head."

The cushion was very soft. The Tsar closed his eyes and Katya began to sing softly. Before long the Tsar fell asleep in his chair ...

When the servants came back, Katya gave them a big chest and told them to put it on the cart.

"My clothes are in there," she said.

"Your clothes are very heavy," said the servants, but they heaved the chest onto the cart. The servants took Katya home.

"It's good to see you, Katya," her father said, but he looked worried. "Why are you back? Did you quarrel with the Tsar?"

"Yes," Katya said. "But don't worry. I won't be back for long."

They heaved the big chest off the cart and took it into the house.

"It's very heavy," Katya's father said. "What's in it?"

"Open the lid and see," said Katya.

The farmer opened the lid of the chest. There inside lay the Tsar, fast asleep.

"What have you done?" the farmer asked. He looked afraid.

Just then the Tsar woke up and saw Katya.

"I thought I told you to go back to your father's house," he said.

"I did," Katya replied.

The Tsar sat up and looked around. He saw Katya's father.

"You wicked girl!" he said to Katya. "How dare you kidnap the Tsar of Russia!"

"Don't you remember your promise?" Katya asked.

"What promise?" asked the Tsar.

"You promised that if you ever got fed up and sent me home I could keep the thing I loved best in the palace. Well, it's you!"

The Tsar laughed. He jumped out of the chest and hugged Katya.

"You were right," he said to the farmer. "Your daughter is the cleverest person in Russia, and I'll never send her away again."